SWANS
- OF THE -
BOUNDARY
WATERS

SWANS
- OF THE -
BOUNDARY
WATERS

- Linda Marie Hilton -

atmosphere press

This is dedicated to the plethora of Ukrainians who have known me since I was gestating in my mother's womb.

They have fixed the cars in my family, taught us, protected us, been our friends, entertained us , been good members of our communities.

Kyiv has existed as a trading center since the fifth century; it was a stop on the trade route from Scandinavia to Constantinople. It has been self-ruled and ruled by Khazars, Vikings, burned to the ground by Mongols more than once, been a part of Lithuania, Poland, and ultimately Russia.

I firmly believe that the Ukraine is a distinct culture within the Slavic Groups and the Ukraine has the right to self-determination and self-government.

ALSO BY
LINDA MARIE HILTON

~

Words of a Feather Hawked Together

TABLE OF CONTENTS

POPULAR CULTURE

GARDENS

SCIENCE

POPULAR
CULTURE

The Potthead Plant

The philodendron repotted every three years
Flourished its leaves and so like the white-tailed deer
Which ran rampant in Westchester County
As NY State will not pay a death bounty
Ensconced in a Back Bay window
With endless room upon a trellis to grow.
Of late its well-heeled owner would smoke
Thereby becoming a much more mellow bloke,
A daily few hits of cannabis
No longer need hid in tony Hyannis.
The philodendron enjoyed the airborne carbon
And then it began to really relish the THC;
It could not wait for the joint to burn:
A truly potthead plant it capriciously came to be.

As the plant inhaled it began to gyre
To dance like Pavlova it did aspire
Its tendrils curled green-sleeved birling bines
Heart shaped leaves take a shine to wine
Winding around until across the mantlepiece
Extended green-sleeves without cease
Surrounding the knickknacks which did not lack
Secret compartments in which to pack
Dried cannabis leaves plastic wrapped well hidden
Once inside the philodendron did root
Inside the owner's awesome now licit loot
Hid behind leaves and a knickknack did
Instead of waiting for the joint to burn
The plant itself did repot in pot not spurned.

To the memories of journeys
by the Red Eye

After the Sunday 10 pm news I await the Red Eye
In an otherwise darkened downtown,
My holiday visit with family now over.
I find my seat, turn off the light, am soon asleep on Sunday night,
Lulled by clickety clack, clickety clack,
No need for a red-eye from the Amtrack bar
(not that they had other than rye and ginger).
Slumbering as the train lumbers through
Rolling countryside as owls hunt far and wide.
At dawn I automatically awake; the window reveals we pass
   across the lake,
Shrouded in mist, our own Avalon (return passage guaranteed).
Then our papers do they check, an hour more to Victoria Station;
The Red Eye delivers me bright eyed, sober, unphotographed,
And not burdened with sleep deprived red eyes.

In the Tunnel

Curled childlike, tumbling, a being in flight
Are you headed into dark or towards the light?
Were you drunk, glued to your cell, now headed to hell,
Tunnel bound has Death now you found.
Has the Matrix curled around you like a shell
The system impenetrable cast iron like a spell.
Deep in conversation did you omit to skite
From a California stop executed pell-mell
Right on red, just keep rolling through
Crosswalks with walkers, bikers, a brew
Of common humanity in sensible shoes.
So now, girl, have you got the moxie to fight
For your health and heartbeat with all your might,
Or shall we call the priest, to give you last rites.

Knott Tea

Dedicated to the Oxford Coma

You may, Knott, take off your striped shirt,
Your bronzed thewy chest to well sport,
Naught but muscle with which to flirt
With what kind gaze? Am I that sort?

You may, Knott, bring me some red wine,
With which to start to tie one on,
Naught but cups to caress so fine,
Begin the beguine so love will dawn.

You may, Knott, encircle my waist,
Bring me close in a sweet slow dance,
Naught between us but sweaty taste,
Scintillating feelings enhanced.

Each night so spent a wee longer
Knotted attraction so much stronger,
A naught, not land, on which to lounge,
Speed in knots yields excuses scrounged.

Naught but theory to guide practice,
Entwine with me , my new love found;
For I was never an actress,
Yet have I now your knot unbound.

When will we ever learn...

Dedicated to the techies who keep not only NLP
*but **The American Scholar** website working!*

If history can teach us any thing or two
It is that when this book unread has rot to earth
Obscurely, despite profundity in its mirth,
The timed out animal cracker cookies to zoo
Ology will go to be studied for their worth
In educating future techies who can do
Whatever to relentlessly reduce the queue
Of failures wrought by cyber creeps which then give birth
To viruses and fungi who then do tackle
Our wretched writings stored within silicon chips,
Reducing our heart-wrested letters to mere snips:
If there were cyber dogs this would raise their hackles.
Thus denied our literary joy of letters,
The Gods remind us how much they are our betters.

From Updike with Love

I am the aristocrat of curves
Which I flaunt with sassy verve.
You are the thewy peasant
With a mien always pleasant.
You may have more money
And while that may buy honey,
It won't shed my peasant blouse
Especially when you grouse
Of the roles men and women
Inevitably must ken,
(even when rolling in the hay,
Rolling in dough makes the day)
So when we into bed do hop
Will you be on bottom or top?

With a copy of Tolkien in my pocket...

Not all who wander are lost,
Some are in love with Jack Frost.
We love to sleep out at night
When the cold begins to bite.
Each morn our army blankets
Are stiff with white hoary coats
Which we roll into our totes.
And off we roam hands in pockets
In search of what has been lost:
Our homes where our word is law,
Though hunger may at us gnaw,
Our freedom won at great cost,
For we the wrong person crossed
And out of our lives we've been tossed.

A Deadly Beauty

Dedicated to the character "James Bond"

Look before you leap
Rivers always run deep.
What you thought was fun:
Horseplay in the sun:
Whitewater hides rocks
Waiting for smart jocks
Jumping on a dare
With chests tanned and bare
Into a fast river
A silver sliver
Plummeting below
The slopes of Mt Stowe,
Frothing in fey spray
Frolicking in play.
The current is strong:
It all goes wrong:
Boy plunges down deep
The current him sweeps
Into murky maws
Damned death has now dawed.
His head a rock strikes,
One with many spikes,
Water he inhales,
A wintery gale.
His friends pull him out
They are all good scouts.
CPR they tried
Then they all did cry:
"Blood gushed from his head
For he was quite dead.
We played, no one was
Supposed to get hurt!"

Home

One's home hugs you and takes you in,
Protects you from accusations of sin
In spite of nefarious furies
Hurling themselves in idiotic frenzies
On a home far from the maddening
Whirlwind rat race of modern life,
A cup of tea, homemade cookies,
A built up fire, roasting chicken,
A sturdy shelter becomes a home
When filled not just with possessions
But scents of personality:
Décor built all of pure whimsy:
"Only she could find all these old things
And garden them to bloom in late spring".
A home is where one's essence blooms
Shown by curated usefulness of rooms.
Color for all sorts of reasons
In celebration of the seasons
Come and then they go: fog, rain, snow:
Which stay outside. Inside we're dry.
When sad we may cry, none will ken,
Our home has hugged us and taken us in.

Insomnia

Chasing lost Lethe I long to sleep,
To sink into slumber aah! So deep!
For in soft darkness my ears hear more,
Yes, even the scabbing o'er a sore,
Repairs of short hairs, broken nails,
My pounding heart as loud as hail.
Even the nightlight dampens sound
And leaves my blankets in a mound.
To toss and turn throughout the night
Yields possible nightmares and leads to fright:
For overreaction takes the day
No joy is found in the simple play
Of a child left alone to run wild
And a natural creature be.
Like tossing on the waves upon the sea
One cannot strive to fall asleep,
Nor can one dive to Lethe's deep depths
But anchorless drift where the current goes
All fast in the clutches of "Oh! I don't know!"
In longing to be flat out dead to the world
A bobbing log tired of being birled
Insomnia shreds logic into threads
And leaves one clinging to one's bed.

Breakfast

The clock of singing birds' chorus slowly brings consciousness to
    the sun
Which sleepily bestirs itself to arise, at first gray, then yellow,
Pale and pinkish then brighter and brighter stretching to ascend
    the sky
To send warm rays through my window to accompany singing
    birds' songs
Gently bringing me from Lethe and sleep to hear leaves against
    my window
'til I follow the sun to make coffee of rich grounds, hot and steaming
With cream and cocoa and cinnamon to slowly savor, nice and hot
'til I can remember how to make pancakes, with syrup and my jam
Made with fruit and apple and honey and naught else, to smother
    pancakes
Or toasted homemade thick sliced sourdough buttered thickly on
    a plate
Which I found at a thrift store, a dainty china painted with flowers
That once were fruit, then jam, then eaten: oh where have all the
    flowers gone?
A second cup of coffee in my moxie java mug while I watch
The clock of singing birds' chorus eat, drink and bathe on my patio
Reminding me to eat my melon, savoring the cool crispness of
Both fruit and morning: my whole day ahead, a blank slate of time
    waiting
For my third cup of coffee to be drunk and the crossword to be
    done.

The Prestige of Veneer

Even the rich and mighty can only afford veneer
In spite of their ability to only drink the right beer
For millenniums appearance has always been paramount
Which is why Ebeneezer Scrooge did nothing but count.
Every article of clothing must always be bespoke
Else one's peers will about one made very nasty jokes.
One's estate and grounds' appearance will fill a certain niche
The yearly upkeep and procurements will fill a microfiche.
Yet for all this fullness owned when one looks within
One sees that one's possessions were taken by a djinn
Leaving only toxic fumes which foul the air in every room
The heights of conspicuous consumption plunge to a ravenous coombe.
In spite of the dust from which we are all created
All these grand accoutrements will cause Gaia to berate us
As though gravity were of absolutely no importance
For we sink in gloom under weight of penurious inheritances.
From deep space extraterrestrials view us as Earth's veneer:
A skin-deep cacophony at which they loudly jeer.

The Colossus

Standing statuesque all day and night
Watching fishermen come and go
I am glad of the clip-ons I've been given
Mon physique mystique est la musique
To all the sea nymphs of the deep
By my stride windward and leeward are riven
Home comers know exactly where to go
Even when fogbound moonless nights obscure their sight
From my shoulder the harbour master observes how low
In the water cargo laden vessels are driven
By oarsmen so strong there is no need to tow
Until dockside they become a welcome sight
Should Venus arise amidst loads of wood
I would dive to mate her, I the Colossus of Rhodes.

Not a Hotel

I'm not a hotel
Magnate's child, just a cousin,
A fifth , not of scotch
But of blood, descendants of
Centuries' William Hiltons'

Finding New England
Grander than Northumberland
With game, fish, and trees
Enough for any fellow
Hardworking enough to live

Off the land so grand:
The New World so brave
The seacoast so wild
And free to be whatever
One wishes to be.

A river runs deep
In one's soul beneath mountains
uplifting one's spirit.

Fabric

Without flowers the fabric
Of life would not be
As no seeds would ever be conceived
So tend your garden and its well
And weave each night a magic spell.

Life on a bicycle

Secure piled gear on bike rack
With colorful bungee cords
Stretched taut.

My back rests my pack
On gear laden rack as I pedal
Towards coffee serving warmth
So I can slowly gently awaken.

My leg over the
Gear piled on my bicycle
Rack, I glide to a stop in
Imitation of a swan,
Gracefully I hope.

I dart hither and yon,
Defying gravity
On a bicycle.

Homeward bound, booty
Balanced on bicycle in
A weight bearing cardio
Workout not for the
Fainted hearted but for the brave.

Velvet

She was the kind of woman who
Ineffably reminded you
Of silky sultry dark velvet
You can pick which jewel tone hue.
She had the poise of Sargent's "Madame X":
Creamy white shoulders, swanny neck,
And curves to knock the sox off Yogi Bera's ilk.
Her voice was low and silky
And how she loved to sing,
She'd lean on the grand piano
Waiting for her pianist to reach
Her bar in a Shubert song,
She knew every one by heart.
Her voice would lift, dip, swell, and fade,
Her performance of the highest grade.
She'd sing a long set
And then caress the pearls at her neck,
And bow with her pianist at them.
They'd mingle with the guests for champagne and caviar,
And little petit fours until it was eleven,
Announced by the grandfather clock's chimes.
Guests would drift out to the door,
Retrieve their cloaks and furs,
Chauffeurs waiting by their pricy cars.
Pianist and contralto went by
The back road out the west way
And home they went,
Enriched a little more and well fed,
Another Saturday night well earned.

Ink

Curses, cursive is no longer taught
With all this modernity what have we wrought?

To Dante

Thank you, Dante, for the plan of hell
Without which we never could tell
Where nefarious individuals
Will evermore linger.
Thank you, Dante, for categorizing sin,
Each penance meted out
To be survived in a hellish din.
Thank you, Dante for putting
Each sin in its place
Designed to put sin in the face
Of the one who committed it.
Thank you, Dante for now I can specifically curse
Those who malign, abuse, and harm
Me for nothing worse
Than who my forbears be
Or what I ate or drank
And where I did these imbibe:
Now I can curse them each
To their rightful place
In Hell.
Thank you, Dante for the vernacular
Each culture may in its own time luxuriate:
Greek and Latin thought do form
A basis upon which variety may flourish.
Thank you, Dante for handing literary arts
To the general public
So their private thoughts and thus
Their minds be freed.
Thoughts may perambulate
Since language structures thought,
Each tongue its own perspective
Of the world may create.
Thank you, Dante for handing mankind
The path with signposts
So much easier to comprehend,
Walking through metaphors
To enlighten enfeebled minds,
Showing the vernacular capable of metaphors

To explicate our acts,
To lift the common soul to a place of erudition.
Thank you, Dante
For showing the vernacular
Capable of showing the way to God.

Rooted deep in Gaia
Mountains beckon us to be
Attuned to the earth.

A Poem Pulls Up

A poem pulls up its sox
It wishes to be syllabist
A poem coasts in neutral
A blank verse waiting to be etched
Each morning poem tries on clothes
To look its daily best
For every day a poem is
(better than being is not)
Sometimes poem pulls on heartstrings
To tie emotions in knots
Other times poem is recited
To celebrate wedding vows
Once in awhile poem is drunk
And becomes ditties and drivel
Sometimes poem is lonely
And mopes about and snivels
For thousands of years poem has been
Our hearts, souls, memories of kin
What would we do without poem
Even in Pippi Longstocking sox!

Self Portrait I

I have told you time and again
That I am neither a thespian
Nor a lesbian
But instead a classical musician,
Trained in music's diction.
To live is not the play
But to live is to love to play
Tunes both bright as day
And as somber as darkest night
Where ne'er does any light
Try to shine bright.
To play is to live,
To play is to love, to coo as a dove
To play is to be alive.
One's playing is one's wife,
One's playing is one's life.

So, How does it Seam?

So what is the mettle in your "seems"
Illusions are shields, not just in dreams.
Braes and coombs present such scenes
Hiding well what it all means.
Hold fast, be staunch, the truth will out,
It needs fresh air lest it become doubt.
As such stitches in sides become side seams
So on Fridays I can perpetually ween.

Self Portrait II

Bodacious elan, now that's my style;
With plenty of verve I'll go the mile
With insouciant guile no need to swerve
'round customers in a file, limned to a man.
Get the job done by the deadline date
Now I'm on a run perhaps to find a mate.
Never to be late, always ahead of the gun,
Always daring fate with a ready pun.
Live life to the fullest, pack every moment,
Words always the truest, fraught feelings never lent,
Counting each hard earned cent, each day the frugalist,
Lest all vivacity be spent, oh! Life is the cruelest!
So I use my curves and all of my verve
To make men swerve to admire my NERVE!

Revisiting America the Beautiful

Oh beautiful for spacious skies
And amber waves of grain

Oh beautiful for mountains high
Traversed by the trains

Oh beautiful for drenching rains
To quench our harvest's thirst
That grow our grasses high
That livestock may eat well

Oh beautiful for forests deep
Old and wisdom laden
With a biome we are
learning to appreciate

Oh beautiful for abundant land
Both in crops and space
That all who come here may
With hard work come to own.

Oh beautiful for Lady Liberty
Her torch and head held high
As planes and boats her now see
while bringing new folks here

Oh beautiful for immense lands
That each ethnicity may new
Lives in enclaves begin to live
Until they learn to all hold hands

Oh beautiful for local schools
That each morn welcome kids
No matter what color ,creed, or race
That each one learn their three R's well

Oh beautiful for fifty states
Each one a different flavor
That each ilk of inhabitants

May some of dear life savor
Each in a different way
Each on a different path
Yet all in commonwealth
And hopefully in good health.

Oh beautiful for opportunity
Each may an Andrew Carnegie be.

Oh beautiful for serious mettle
None should a fight with us pick
For we will fight with all our might
Our way of life to defend.

Oh beautiful for traditions past
From Pilgrims' Hats to wonton soup
From ptarmigan to paella
Smoked fish baked into bread
Couscous to serve with lamb
And don t forget the coco yam.

Oh beautiful we found this land
We think we possess it
Now let us show it some respect
Let us listen to those who were
Here long before Caucasians

Let us stifle our greedy opinions
Let us live in harmony ,
No matter where we're from,
With what God has given us

After all, Earth is our sole home.

Pizza

Pizza is my favorite food
It puts me in the best of moods
Bread and cheese, tomato bright!
Ah! What a lovely sight.
To happiness it does allude,
It proves that I am not a prude
But an epicure in many ways
Delighting in the living all the days.
Appetites need not be crude
Nor should they put me on a rood
Variety of toppings ,spices might
Just fend off the most awful fight
With my latest hunk called "Dude",
Like playing music on an oud.

GARDENS

A garden fragment

To garden is to receive pardon
For the errors of human ways
To garden is to nurture
And for our incursions pay

To garden is to acknowledge
We need permission to stay
To earth we are all midges
Who on this earth do play.

Random

Random seeds strewn
Randomly , never in lines,
Wind whirled patternless
Where ever the seed
When tired and in need
Of a nap in the sun,
Or to be cached in a crevice.
Springtime always reinforces
Nature's tendency: forests
Of abundance without redundance
Of an Euclidean geometry
Save the plants themselves
Each having selected
A leaf shape, petal arrangement
While distribution of types
Remains uncategorical
Defying mere mortals comprehension.

The Speed of Roses

The tempo of a wild rose
Along a country road
Covering well a retaining wall
Filling in nooks and crannies
Like jam on an English muffin,
Holding in place with tendrils green
Hiding mossy patches
With leaves: serrated ovals,
Multitudinous blooms.
All summer long producing hips for tea.
Measured by a few centimeters a day
Accelerating after a summer rain,
Slowing in a droughty August,
Marking the passage of summer time
By length of days and Orion's Belt.
Roots aiming for a damp spot
Far into the bank, the wall holds,
Is it distance gone or time well spent?
The tempo of a wild rose
Keeps time with Earth herself
Marking rotations, orbits made;
Nature holding itself in place.

Evoke the Wind

Paint the wind
As evidenced by birling leaves
Without chlorophyll
Sighing with relief
At the task of summer heat

color the wind
see where the rain drops go
leaves, windows, bicycle seats,
plaster the leaves
like wallpaper on windshields

stroke in the wind
clamp the paper to the easel
wield the brush like a pro
paint in the birling leaves
as evidence the wind blows.

The Tenses of Tensionlessness

Thyme flowers amongst boulders,
All tenses unspool.
Muscles melt in the sun:
Here and now was at dawn
Cool and refreshed,
Here and now melatonin rises
To lie just beneath the skin's surface
Catching ultraviolet
Holding it fast as the skin holds it,
Gulliver's filaments to bind us to earth
Unspooled from the present
Repurposed to be the day's captive
Until gloaming brings shivers
Now that sunlight has withered.
Time has flourished.
Thyme has furbished a backdrop,
Scented the present, will scent the future,
Unwound from minute seeds,
Minute by minute, hourly stretching,
Reaching to the sun, spooling the year,
For past, present, and future to hear:
Gravity's thong while cesium quakes,
Chores undone, Ma will berate:
Thyme flowers amongst boulders
Home we go with sunburnt shoulders.

A Frostly Echo

A square impromptu

At ten o' clock we saw snow in spring
Ten inches deep, winter's chill it brings.
OH! Clock of seasons where are you now,
Ghosted away from Hyla Brooks brow?
A net of ents ten deep will snow keep
From drifting o'er spring peaks out of snow,
Not yet with summer's strengths fully strong,
Spring's vibrant hues a paled paper sheet,
As we walk and talk this "winter's" eve.

......when an elf leaves Middle Earth......

Who will the west wind bring tonight?
A stag bearing the fey elf king?
In search of a child home to bring
Beyond the reach of any brave knight?
Will this child cease to be?
Could wonderment at elfin lands
Built deep amongst towering stands
Of trees from which an eagle sees
Ennoble his mind at this good Fortune
Smiling gently on this good fate,
His mother outraged, in grief awaits,
Her tears flowing fill a lagoon,
Her human frailty cannot fight.
Who will the elfking take tonight?

Whither one goes in
Fall flora will lose heart, then
Cold will them wither.

Coulter's Globemallow,
a Sonoran Native

Seeds born by wind
or tucked amongst an eagle's feathers
Northward journey: an adventure
Onto eroded lava vent cones
Ranged along the Rocky Mountain Uplift
Against all odds of climate extremes
Nested in sun baked sandstone crumbs
Alone atop a beige ridge
Tenaciously growing and blooming
In spite of all the tribulations, a
Very nice surprise for the hiker, an
Excellent inspiration to carry on!

SCIENCE

Plant

Plant is green
Blue sky / ocean mixed with
Yellow sun
Air, water, sun,
Earth has begun
Earth has begun to live
Some earth has become life
Now who did Cronus
Take as his wife?

The Poetry of Science

There is beauty in the atoms,
In the way the electrons spin,
And since poetry is beauty,
Science is poetry and beauty both,
Look at the periodic chart
But not in the dark
But in light of sun lit day
And contemplate how our sun
May fuse elements up to iron
So who makes the cobalt?
How do we stay so easily upright
As we hurl through space both day and night?
So what is a graviton anyways?
Does it traverse inner space ways?
Do symmetrons exist in space?
Are the domain walls in pathways?
Since particles rhyme
With the ease of a dime
Are they the essence of poetry,
The sound waves of words?
Or do we exist
In simultaneous sorts of worlds?

Train Time

Like a locomotive going from cold rest to full hot steam
A woman goes into labor:
Water breaking, contractions over hours,
Dilation, more contractions
Yielding a babe whose first wail
Echoes a train whistle.
Then life chugs on.
Its time measured by the quivering
Of a cesium atom so precise
It divides time into slices
So minute thousands fit well in
To a minute of sixty seconds.
A seed lies in the ground all winter
Until rain and sun warmed earth
Wake it from its months long slumber.
All knowledge it needs contained in a bead
Nondescript yet full of worth
To yield flowers or a towering oak.
So cesium quivers and never stops
Babe after babe born without cease
Plants sprout and grow and go to seed
Cesium quivers:
A train of never-ending motions called time.

Our Moon in our Galaxy

The iamb pulse of our hearts
Does it echo pulsars light years away?
Where was the moon before Earth captured her?
Or does she want our waters for herself?
Where is our place in the galaxy's chart?
Why need we cesium to calculate the day?
In the cold light of the moon let us wear fur
We creatures of Gaia have enormous wealth.

Elementally

Earth and water are solid
Air and fire have no substance
Earth, a couch potato, water runs,
Air billows, wafts, winds, seeps
All in and about solid earth
Whipping liquid water to joyous
Molecules no longer bound by the meniscus
Fire has neither shape, substance, nor solidity
As its flames feed on carbon based flora
Occasionally roasting fauna
An acid or lye will eat away any solid
By grabbing stray electrons
Water will act as an eternal tumbler
Polishing all surfaces of solids
Fire has no electrons, therefore no substance
Yet it vanquishes all life in its path.

Grain of Sand

Each grain of sand is a speck of time
Having counted eighty thousand
Wind and water have created
One thousand seventeen more grains
Each time I think I've counted all
Wind and water pile up more sand
While volcanoes belch more rocks to grind.
Since sand is infinite so is
Time as it ticks ever forwards,
Gnashing hiccups in just knotty
Limits making nether ovoid
Parabolas quicken rambling
Somewhere tumultuously under
Veritable white xenophobes
Yet Zorro will arrive before
Calamity does edge frothing
Instead danger is a sand grain
Blown by the wind tumbled by streams
Beached by oceans keeping good times.

Without

Inside the box it's
Too square: the pattern's known, none
Ever work within the norms.
In unknown beyond
Solutions seekers will find.

Bioluminescence

Glow with the essence of life
Emit endorphins like tweets on a fife
Greet each day as a set of moments ripe
To be played upon by Pan with his pipes
Ignore everything which does your heart rile
Push away that which causes digestive bile
Let light be gathered by your glinting eyes
Reflect, refract, on what and where and why
Ponder all that resides on our earth by our sides
Going around and around on an everlasting ride
Let the glow of your soul be a bottomless bowl
A tiny fraction of our good old Sol
No life form is ugly as long as it glows
Multitasking complex chemical reactions
Which cannot be reduced to simple fractions
So glow with the essence of life
Since not only does each life matter
But all glowing life matters.

My own Geometry

The geometry of my childhood
Was entirely Euclidean
Ninety degree square buildings
of Brookline, walks round the reservoir.
I grew up in suburbia
Quarter acre well treed plots;
I grew up and rewilded
To a distant urban place,
Found my first lagrange point
And flung myself out
Far beyond the nest of my upbringing.
The second LaGrange point brings me back in
But just somewhat,
Still within reach of kith and kin.
So Christmas consists of a tree
And stockings hung with care;
Easter blesses us with colored eggs;
Outside hamburgers for the Fourth of July.
I do not actually want
To venture to Deep Space Nine,
Even though I insist on freedom,
I needn't bolt to the stars.

Deep Learning

So we delve more deeply
Into how crystals form
We study 'til we're sleepy
To ascertain chemical norms
The more we see
The less we comprehend
The more we perceive
Drives us to wit's end
As our knowledge deepens
Our awe becomes exponential
So what is knowledge anyways
But memory and recognition
That we live out our days
On the edge of a premonition.

An Ode to the Moon

Moonlight fills my hand
But yet I do not hold it
Moonlight fills a valley
But yet earth does not grasp it
The light that is illuminates
The gravity of the situation
Of the tides perambulation
Does the moon wish our waters
Or do waters wish to moon
But I have to tell you
We will not know this soon.

Triptych of Water

In the beginning

Gurgle. Bubble. Lines of bubbles. Over a volcanic vent: boil,
boil, toil and trouble, cauldron of the ocean burn and bubble:
seethe with ions grabbing here and there, let us see what molecules
evolve: slowly come together as chains of this and that until one
lovely RNA strand forms, then another, and another. Float in
the ocean, froth here and there. Volcanos make islands, larger
and larger they grow.
The moon wanting our seas pulls water from side to side until it
sloshes over the new land. Over and over this happens until the
RNA learns to stay itself, making a bubble dry on the outside, wet
on the inside. The moon does this for eons: does she want our
water or is she the source of life: the goddess?
Or a mechanism designed by a galactic power to water the new
land until lichens emerge, and fungi, clinging to rocks. The seas
as a vast swimming pool of life. Strands of RNA are zapped by
lightening and become more complex and algae emerge. They
cling to rocks and strand more into seaweeds . eons of this increase
the variety of diatoms, protozoa, until jellyfish emerge. Water
as the primordial soup is the basis for all life. Life crawls out onto
land. Plants grow taller and eat all the carbon dioxide, spewing
out oxygen and putting the carbon into their beings. Life crawls
over plants and eats them.
The seas have spawned an entire planet of an infinite variety of life.

Master Carvers who have
Terraformed the Earth

Playing In the air, riding the wind, crystalizing on airborne spores
to fall maybe as snow to lie in the sun or find a narrow defile and
congregate merrily with our kin and tumble downhill gurgling,
frothing, jumping into the air with glee or to be bottle green and
swirl gently in a cool shady eddy beneath which trout nap. We
made the Grand Canyon, we made The Three Gorges, we roam
from Nepal to Nairobi.
The sand and silt we have worn away we leave here and there as
alluvial deposits so that plants may grow and other creatures will
have food to eat. We shape the valleys for shelter from withering
winter winds. We break rocks into pieces, and pieces into pieces,
and so on until there is dirt and the occasional diamond for wonder.
We let gold settle out since it is so heavy into the placer layers.
We nourish the plants. We give birds baths. We gently wash
gravel beds so salmon may spawn and fish may be born. We are
the spouts of whales. We are the currents hot and cold adding to
the Coriolis effect so that there may be variations in the weather.
We travel underground here and there, sometimes resting so
humans can find us when they dig wells. Sometimes we go deep
enough to heat up and jump joyously as Old Faithful. Sometimes
we just burble to the surface and don't freeze in winter so creatures
can drink and do not have to eat snow. Or we form a heated
pool for bathing. We love to be waterfalls above all else: such
playing! At Niagara we positively thunder in our glee.
We exist at all temperatures on Terra in one or another of our
forms. At 32 degrees F we can exist in all three forms: gas, liquid,
and solid, in close proximity. We are water unless electricity is
applied to us to break us into hydrogen and oxygen: We are
Water!!!!

My Love is Blue Water

Zygote, in my bubble, I bounce in water blue, blue, blue my
   world is blue,
blue as the sky, one seventh of refracted light. Like all terran life,
   I begin in
water blue, blue, blue my world is blue. Plain water, algal water,
   sulphurous
water, blue, blue my world is blue. Small and light I float on blue
   water, blue, blue
my world is blue. Love is blue. Like two water molecules: my
   head and arms
are one, my torso and legs are the second. Imitation is the sincerest
   form of
flattery. Oxygen is staunch: head and torso. Hydrogen flails:
   arms and legs.
Blue, blue my world is blue. I am a two molecule chain of water.
Eventually I am big and I am 89% sea water, I enclose my world,
   my blue world
with just 11 % of stuff, mostly carbon. My bag of surrounding
   water bursts and
after much stress I am born into air, no water, so I cry!!!! I cry
   for water. All my
life I will cry for water. When I am mature I will cry for 80 ounces
   a day. Without
You blue water, I dry, I sere, I become a heap of calcium, blue,
   blue my world is
blue, longing for you, now I am without life.

City of Stars

We live in a city of stars
Each star way station far apart
To get from one to another
We lack a monorail
Our minds so underdeveloped
We cannot build a light sail
We've no notion of how
Space travel could carry us
Beyond the techniques
Of medieval catapults
Which let us use LaGrange points
To position our best telescopes
We live in a city of stars
Our own star enables our lives
Those among us who excel
We label as "bright little stars"
We live in a city of stars
That populates the universe
This universe expands into what?
That 's beyond the scope of this verse.

TO
The Hamlet
of
IS and IS NOT

Reflections on a Photo

Since one can see a cloud, it is;
Since one can sail through it, it is not;
Since one can see a reflection, it is;
Cloud disappears into rings of ripples, it is not;
A hamlet is; Hamlet, being fiction is not;
A mountain in a photograph is;
Just not in Denmark.
Denmark contains hamlets, which are
And even Hamlet , who is not.
English has always contained the quantum leap.

Essay

On Diversity

So what does tolerant really mean? "that which a Catholic accepts?" (catholic meaning tolerant, ie, accepting of Jews, Gentiles, Samaritans, Zeusites, Zoroastrians, Hindi, and followers of Ishtar).
So I, having four grandparents each of a different faith(Catholic, Methodist, Baptist, Episcopalian), as a baby boomer, born into this country's most affluent era, ought to be considered progressive. So why are a goodly number of my fellow Catholics (hereafter referred to a "Tolerants" so upset that I am different than they? Why is it that in the city of Baltimore the "Tolerant" parishes are set up as follows:
(this was told to me by one who grew up there): Irish parishes, German parishes, Italian parishes......
then parishes for couples who intermarry: a parish for german-irish marriages, one for italian-irish marriages, etc.   This was done to quell fighting.   Let us go to any rural area in this country. Farmer/ranchers know the rules of genetics, they follow them well when they breed livestock or pets.   Yet they resent an outsider courting their women, even though they know in the long run that is better for
the genetic makeup of the children resulting of those unions.
If I go back three generations in my family, the ethnic groups are: American, all the four parts of Britain, Slovak, Polish.
Going back 6 more generations yields: British being broken down to Welsh, Scots, English, Cornish.
American breaks down to English, scots, welsh, irish, Cornish, Canadian.   Canadian breaks down to both
English speaking and French speaking Canadian and native American, the tribe which is now known as the Passamaquoddy.   Also in there somewhere are dutch and german traders.   The Slovak and Polish break down to anyone who took refuge in the Carpathian Mountains.   Those forbears have been Christian
since before 850 AD.   So why is it so terrible that I represent genetic diversity?   Why is it so terrible that I have migrated across this continent?   America was founded by people who for the most part were discontent with some part of their lives.   They sought the right to own land, be prosperous, marry who they

chose, worship as they chose. They had gumption to pay to cross the Atlantic Ocean in wooden boats propelled by the wind in their sails, often a good two months voyage.

Those who come to our shores may in general worship as they chose, we forbid certain practices, such as the binding of women's feet, burning a widow alive with her dead husband, polygamy, sacrifices of any live creature. We forbid cruelty to animals, forced arranged marriages, child labor, and many other practices which were once common on a global level.

The Bill of Rights guarantees the right of the people to assemble peaceably. This means that people may gather to worship, watch a sporting event, attend a marriage, funeral, or graduation ceremony. They may assemble to partake of a musical performance or for tournaments in chess, tennis, or cribbage. Furthermore they do not need to eat or drink any particular beverage or eat any particular food to have this right. This right extends to having their mail and packages delivered, either by the USPS, UPS, or other carrier. This is considered professional behavior. We strive to practice the golden rule whether we believe in God or not. We eschew violence as a means of settling disputes.

If one were to look through my life one would see that the men I have dated are also "mixtures." My close friends are "mixtures". I choose people who are tolerant of diversity. I choose people who are kind and considerate. I value politeness and professionalism. The food and beverages people consume are not signals and rarely mean anything. We do not make diabetics eat donuts, heart attack victims eat fried chicken, or those with ulcers consume very acidic foods.

So why must I, in order to prove that I am "tolerant" put up with people who are "intolerant" being rammed down my throat? I am not a guinea pig so see if various individuals can behave themselves. If we as a nation wish to address problems of inequities among various marginalized groups, we must as a whole stop being upset because this, that, or the other individual is "different". Those who come to America as immigrants must understand that we are different because we tried to leave those societal constraints we chafed against behind and create a truly New World.

MEMORIES
OF A
SUMMER

On being upcountry

Wild Idaho

Free flowing rivers
Rugged mountain wilderness
Teeming flora and fauna
Wild, wild Idaho
Flourishing in nature's realm.

....

Huge white cumuli
Skate across the cold hardness
Of the clear blue sky leaving
A wake of pure white
Mist trailing like a Bride's veil.

....

Horseshoe Bend

Free from the gorge the
River meanders in large
Loops suddenly sedate
In nature's southernmost
Valley of the Boise Front.

....

Ridge trail high above
Flood waters madly surging
Rocks tumbling into scree piles
Worn by Shoshones'
Seasonal arduous trek.

....

When I am hungry
You are closed, when I've just dined
You are open, buffalo
Burgers and fixins
Can't we get it together?

Smith's Ferry

Suddenly widens
The canyon, placid is the
Usually turbulent flume
Shallows dotted with
Peacefully grassy hummocks.

The Big Eddy

Bottle green water pauses
On its way to the sea to
Whirl around a clear deep pool
To hide speckled trout
Before forming white water.

Poor peeling plastered
Narrow arched span across the
Racing Payette River hangs
On despite heavy
Thundering ceaseless traffic.

Gasping from climbing
Past the rainbow bridge the road
Bursts into the meadow of
Round Valley, peaceful
Level circle of broad fields.

West mountain's ridge heaves
Steeply, good only for goats
Ski trails and towering trees
Due north-south topped with
Ancient Shoshone foot trail.

....

Iron fists of the wind
Whipped through dark nimbuses to
Shred purple like feathers
Of a fancy bird to
Gauzy wisps at cloud's edges.

The bunkhouse's crick

The snow melt filled rill
Murmurs under trees, over
Rocks strewn by glaciers, reaching
Grassy slopes filled with
Camus and placid fat cows.

....

Morning's chill grips like
That of November til mid
Morning's sun chases coolness
To forest shade from
The solstice's blazing sun.

The snow just melted
Grass starts greening up to sun
Drinking frost each chill morning
Calling to aspens
Up spring sego lily blooms.

Bright blue lake headed
North to a horizon's deep
Purple mountain on a bright
Orange fading to
Yellows, then twilight's white.

A lone pink cloud aflame
Of bright pink and dark purple
Billows skyward plumed against
A palest blue sky
At the edge of twilight's dawn.

....

Sleepy, I kill the
Radio crooning sweet tunes,
The silence is deadly so
I wonder if my
Ears work "til an owl swoops.

....

The river roars 'neath
Rainbow Bridge as cars begin
A twisty journey south by
Foamy water's rush
Through a narrow ravine.

....

Humungous heat puffed
Cumuli are parked over
The Boise Front, sentinels
Against breezes which
Lessen summer's baking heat.

....

OUR SOL HOME
IS EARTH

NOTES

Frontispiece:
Drawn by the author using Adobe Illustrator software

Knott Tea:
Comment: the first three stanzas were posted to NLP 27 April 2019.
The prompt was to write a seduction poem not using the first
person singular and to include a negative somehow. The fourth and
fifth stanzas have been added to extend the pun.
Comment two: this is dedicated to one of the four English teachers
who taught the A P English class I was in my junior and senior years
in high school. Said individual, now over 90 no doubt and possibly
living in a place was of the opinion that females are rarely good at
punning.

From Updike with Love:
The NLP prompt was a particular paragraph in Updike's novel
Couples.

A Deadly Beauty:
The NLP prompt was to include the phrase "no one was supposed
to get hurt".

Insomnia:
I wrote this after reading Benjamin's book of the same name.

Breakfast:
Included in Saint Gabriel Valley Poetry Quarterly issue # 56
I wrote this to submit to a journal which had requested poems about
Breakfast, and no haikus please, something more substantial.
So I wrote this "square meal", 17 lines of 17 syllables each, a haiku
"squared".
That journal did not appreciate my humor but Kingfisher did.

The Prestige of Veneer:
Written after reading a similar poem by Walter Harris III

Life on a Bicycle:
Included in Saint Gabriel Valley Poetry Quarterly issue # 61

Velvet:
Inspired by a poem by Ingrid Burch
I used the title as the first line and my pen went in its own direction.

To Dante:
Written in commemoration of the seven hundredth anniversary of
Dante's death in 1321.

A Poem Pulls Up:
Inspired by a poem of the same name by Clive Grewcock

Random:
Inspired by the poem "Random" by R Srivastava

Evoke the Wind:
Inspired by a poem posted to Spillwords
Which contains the words ":I am painting the wind…"

The Poetry of Science:
Inspired by a poem by Aurora Kastanias

Train Time:
Inspired by the poem "Train of Life" by M Dziwisz.

Elementally:
Inspired by "Wildfires" by Shih-Fang Wang

Grain of Sand:
Inspired by a poem of a similar name by
R William Standish on the sand in a desert.

Bioluminescence:
After a poem by the same name by P Tran.

My Own Geometry:
Written in response to a prompt listed in Poets and Writer's Magazine

Deep Learning:
Inspired by a poem by the same name by Ryann Stevenson

An Ode to the Moon:
Inspired by a poem of the same name by Boris Simonovski

My Love is Blue Water
This last paragraph was inspired by the lyrics from Paul Mauriat's song "Love is Blue".

City of Stars
Inspired by the poem by A A Phuong "On the Road"

Photo by Alex Murzin posted to Unsplash
I tweaked it in Canva

ACKNOWLEDGEMENTS

The following poems were published in the *Saint Gabriel Valley Poetry Quarterly:*

"Breakfast", "Self Portrait I", and" Life on a Bicycle".

The following poems were written for and posted to the *Next Line Please* poetry blog hosted by *The American Scholar* website:

"The Potthead Plant", "To the Memories of Journeys by the Red Eye", "Knott Tea", "When will we ever Learn", "A Deadly Beauty", "Not a Hotel", "Self Portrait I", "A Frostly Echo", and "….When an elf leaves Middle Earth….".

ABOUT ATMOSPHERE PRESS

Atmosphere Press is an independent, full-service publisher for excellent books in all genres and for all audiences. Learn more about what we do at atmospherepress.com.

We encourage you to check out some of Atmosphere's latest releases, which are available at Amazon.com and via order from your local bookstore:

Melody in Exile, by S.T. Grant

Covenant, by Kate Carter

Near Scattered Praise Lies Our Substantial Endeavor, by Ron Penoyer

Weightless, Woven Words, by Umar Siddiqui

Journeying: Flying, Family, Foraging, by Nicholas Ranson

Lexicon of the Body, by DM Wallace

Controlling Chaos, by Michael Estabrook

Almost a Memoir, by M.C. Rydel

Throwing the Bones, by Caitlin Jackson

Like Fire and Ice, by Eli

Sway, by Tricia Johnson

A Patient Hunger, by Skip Renker

Lies of an Indispensable Nation: Poems About the American Invasions of Iraq and Afghanistan, by Lilvia Soto

The Carcass Undressed, by Linda Eguiliz

Poems That Wrote Me, by Karissa Whitson

Gnostic Triptych, by Elder Gideon

For the Moment, by Charnjit Gill

Battle Cry, by Jennifer Sara Widelitz

I woke up to words today, by Daniella Deutsch

Never Enough, by William Guest

Second Adolescence, by Joe Rolnicki

ABOUT THE AUTHOR

Born and raised in Massachusetts, blue-eyed Linda Marie Hilton dreamed of being an oboist in a symphony orchestra. Studying oboe in NYC a year, then running out of money, she worked as an accounting clerk, returning to night school to obtain a BSc in Accounting from CUNY. She worked several years in public accounting and in the evenings played her oboe in a community orchestra. She moved to the Pacific Northwest for her health and has lived there more than 25 years. Once again starving she became a poet. She enjoys reading, writing, gardening, hiking, knitting, designing and crocheting beaded lace, the beautiful wilderness, bicycling, and being a practical environmentalist.

Made in the USA
Columbia, SC
16 August 2024